The Jamestown
□ Wit

Drawing Conclusions

Second Edition   Advanced Level

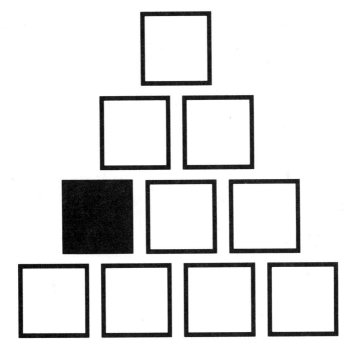

Jamestown Publishers
Providence, Rhode Island

Comprehension Skills Book

Second Edition

No. 184 Drawing Conclusions
Advanced Level

© 1974, 1993 by Jamestown Publishers, Inc.

This edition was prepared with the editorial assistance of Kraft & Kraft

Cover and text design by Thomas Ewing Malloy

Printed in the United States of America

3 4 5 6 7 8   99 98 97 96

ISBN 0-89061-617-5

Readability
Parts One and Two, Lesson: Level K
Part Three, Sample Exercise: Level G
Part Four, Practice Exercises: Levels H–L
Passages 1–6: Level H   Passages 7–12: Level I
Passages 13–18: Level J   Passages 19–24: Level K
Passages 25–30: Level L

INTRODUCTION

The Comprehension Skills Series has been prepared to help students develop specific reading comprehension skills. Each book is completely self-contained. There is no separate answer key or instruction manual. Throughout the book, clear and concise directions guide the student through the lessons and exercises.

The titles of the Comprehension Skills books match the labels found on comprehension questions in other Jamestown text-books. The student who is having difficulty with a particular kind of question can use the matching Comprehension Skills book for extra instruction and practice to correct the specific weakness.

Each book in the Comprehension Skills Series is divided into five parts.

1. Explanation: Part One clearly defines, explains, and illustrates the specific skill.

2. Instruction: Part Two offers an interesting and informative lesson presented in clear, readable language. A preview technique used regularly throughout Parts One and Two requires the student to anticipate and respond.

3. Sample Exercise: Part Three consists of a sample exercise with questions. For each question, the thinking of a student who answers correctly is modeled, the correct answer is explained, and the shortcomings of the other answers are pointed out. The sample exercise is designed to prepare the student for the work required in the following section. Students are urged to consult the instructor if they need extra help before proceeding to Part Four.

4. Practice Exercises: Part Four contains thirty practice exercises with questions. Edward Fry's formula for estimating readability was used to sequence the exercises. The passages begin at level H and advance gradually to level L. Students are advised to complete the thirty practice exercises thoughtfully and carefully.

5. Writing Activities: Part Five contains writing activities that help students apply the skills they have learned in earlier parts of the book. Many activities encourage students to work cooperatively with other students.

HOW TO USE THIS BOOK

1. Read Part One, Understanding Conclusions, which begins on page 5. Complete the Preview Quiz as you read.

2. Read Part Two, Drawing a Conclusion, which begins on page 7. Complete the Preview Quizzes as you read.

3. Complete the Sample Exercise in Part Three, which begins on page 15. Read and follow the instructions carefully. After you have completed the exercise, read the explanation following it.

4. Complete the thirty Practice Exercises in Part Four, which begins on page 19. Read and follow the instructions carefully.

5. Complete the Writing Activities, which begin on page 51. Read and follow the instructions carefully. After you complete each activity, your teacher may want to discuss your answers with the class.

6. Use the Answer Key, which begins on page 59, to correct your answers after you complete each exercise.

7. Record your progress on the chart on the inside back cover.

PART ONE

Understanding Conclusions

Preview Quiz 1

As a preview of what will be discussed in Part One, try to answer this question:

What is a conclusion?
- ☐ a. a decision about the outcome that certain conditions will produce
- ☐ b. a decision about the cause of a certain outcome
- ☐ c. a decision about the credibility of an argument

Begin reading Part One to discover how conclusions are different from other types of decisions.

A writer does not always state clearly and directly all the information he or she wishes to communicate. A writer may leave some things unsaid because the writer expects that you, the reader, will draw the proper conclusion on your own. In other cases things go unsaid because the writer is writing for a purpose somewhat different from the reader's purpose for reading. The writer leaves things unsaid—even though he or she understands them to be true—simply because these things are not specifically pertinent to the writer's purpose in writing. You, the reader, must draw your own conclusions in order to reach an understanding suitable to *your* purposes. This is why you need to know how to draw accurate conclusions when you are reading.

What is a conclusion? A conclusion is a decision about the probable effects of certain conditions. To see what a reasonable and sound conclusion is, first read the paragraph that begins on the next page.

The drought and heat wave that have plagued western South Dakota show no signs of abating. Forests in the Black Hills are dangerously dry. Record temperatures are likely to continue for at least another week, say long-range forecasters at the National Weather Service. Health officials caution that extreme temperatures make work and exercise much more difficult, especially for older people and people with a history of heart disease.

Based on the information in this paragraph and on general knowledge about weather, fire, and health, a reader can draw several reasonable conclusions.

Because we know that South Dakota has had a drought and that the drought is expected to continue, we can conclude that people in the area should not waste water.

From the fact that forests in the Black Hills are dangerously dry, we can conclude that campers in the Black Hills should use extreme caution with campfires.

The paragraph points out the dangers of extreme temperatures, especially for older people and people with a history of heart disease. It also states that high temperatures are likely to continue for a week. From that information, we can conclude that older people and people with a history of heart disease should avoid unnecessary exercise during the coming week.

Each of these is a reasonable conclusion based on general knowledge and on the information in the paragraph.

PART TWO

Drawing a Conclusion

Preview Quiz 2

As a preview of what will be discussed next, try to answer this question:

What is a cause-and-effect relationship?
- ☐ a. a relationship in which it is impossible to decide why events occur
- ☐ b. a relationship that cannot be described accurately
- ☐ c. a relationship in which one event makes another happen

Continue reading to discover the correct answer.

The first step in drawing a conclusion is to recognize potential cause-and-effect relationships in what you read. A great deal of logical thinking is based on cause-and-effect relationships. We know from experience that certain events cause others; in other words, certain causes imply certain effects. A rainstorm wets the pavement. The rainstorm is the cause; wet pavement is the effect. Wet pavement makes automobile tires slip. This time, wet pavement is the cause; slipping is the effect. Falling rain implies wet pavements, and wet pavements imply slippery conditions.

There are other ways to state these cause-and-effect relationships. A writer expressing them might do so in any of the following ways:

> Because rain is falling, the pavement will get wet.
> Rain is falling; therefore, the pavement will get wet.
>
> Since the pavement is wet, the tires will slip.
> The pavement is wet, so the tires will slip.

Often, however, writers omit the effects. They state the cause, but merely imply the effect. Therefore, your first step in drawing a conclusion is to decide which statements imply certain results. Consider the statements in the following paragraph:

> Why do some birds migrate while others stay at home all winter? Most birds that migrate do so not because they dislike cold weather but because food is harder to find in cold weather. Seeds are available all the year round, but many insects hibernate during winter. One American bird, the dickcissel of the Midwest, a member of the finch family, is an eater of grasshoppers and locusts. It winters in Central and South America. In contrast, the house sparrow, another member of the finch family, is a seed-eater with a short, sturdy bill that is ideally suited to cracking seeds.

Notice some facts that imply certain outcomes:

> Seeds are available all the year round, . . .
> Many insects hibernate during winter. . . .
> The house sparrow . . . is a seed-eater, . . .

These are causes, but the writer has left their effects unstated. From the information in the rest of the paragraph, we can see certain effects that these causes imply:

> Seeds are available all the year round, so **birds that eat seeds do not have to migrate.**

> Many insects hibernate during winter; therefore, **birds that eat insects must travel to warmer climes where insects are active.**

> Because the house sparrow is a seed-eater, **the house sparrow does not have to migrate.**

8

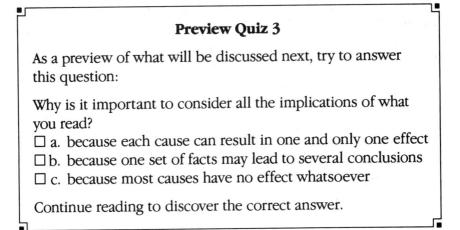

Preview Quiz 3

As a preview of what will be discussed next, try to answer this question:

Why is it important to consider all the implications of what you read?
- ☐ a. because each cause can result in one and only one effect
- ☐ b. because one set of facts may lead to several conclusions
- ☐ c. because most causes have no effect whatsoever

Continue reading to discover the correct answer.

A single cause may produce several effects. Therefore, one set of facts may lead to several conclusions. Because this is so, it is important to consider a range of possible effects before settling on a conclusion. This raises an important point about reading: good readers are actively engaged with the material they are reading, always thinking about it, considering it, weighing it, trying to decide where it leads, what it suggests, and what it implies. Good readers keep an open mind and do not jump to conclusions. Instead, they stretch their thinking and consider all the implications before settling on the most likely conclusion or conclusions.

To see how important it is to consider all the implications, read the following paragraph, which outlines some of the events leading to World War I. As you read, pay particular attention to potential cause-and-effect relationships.

By 1908 tension in Europe was becoming alarming. The French were firmly opposed to Germany, which had annexed Alsace and part of Lorraine after the Franco-Prussian War. Serbia and Russia supported the efforts of Slavs to break free from the Austro-Hungarian Empire and create a Slavic nation. Germany was expanding its empire in the Middle East, where Great Britain had long-standing interests. Earlier, Germany had formed an alliance with Russia and Austria-Hungary, but in

9

1871 Germany turned from Russia and formed a
Dual Alliance with Austria-Hungary alone; later
Italy joined them. France needed allies to oppose
this formidable Triple Alliance.

Many statements in the paragraph are causes that imply certain
effects. Following are some of them, with the word *because* added
to each, to indicate that it is a potential cause:

Because Serbia and Russia supported the efforts of
Slavs to break free from the Austro-Hungarian
Empire. . . .

Because Germany was expanding its empire in the
Middle East, where Great Britain had long-standing
interests. . . .

Because Germany turned from Russia and formed a
Dual Alliance with Austria-Hungary alone. . . .

Because France needed allies to oppose this
formidable Triple Alliance. . . .

What effects do these causes imply? Try to think of as many as
you can. Review the paragraph. Brainstorm. Jot down a list of
potential effects; you will evaluate them in the next section.

As a preview of what will be discussed next, try to answer this question:

Within a paragraph, how are the causes and effects likely to be related?

☐ a. They will not be related.

☐ b. Each cause-and-effect relationship will be separate from any of the others.

☐ c. They will be interrelated.

Continue reading to discover the correct answer.

Because most writing is organized by topic, theme, and idea, you are likely to find that there is a network of causes and effects, not just a simple straight line. When you see the interrelationships of these causes and effects, you may see how they lead to an overall conclusion. At the end of the last section, you listed possible effects of causes mentioned in a paragraph about World War I. Your list of possible effects may have included these:

> **Because** Serbia and Russia supported the efforts of Slavs to break free from the Austro-Hungarian Empire . . .
>
> > Austria-Hungary opposed Serbia.
> > Austria-Hungary opposed Russia.
> > Slavs in Austria-Hungary supported Serbia.
> > Slavs in Austria-Hungary supported Russia.
>
> **Because** Germany was expanding its empire in the Middle East, where Great Britain had long-standing interests . . .
>
> > Great Britain opposed Germany.
> > Middle-Eastern countries opposed Germany.
>
> **Because** Germany turned from Russia and formed a Dual Alliance with Austria-Hungary alone . . .
>
> > Russia opposed Germany.
> > Russia opposed Austria-Hungary.

As you consider these effects, you should begin to see a pattern emerging. Germany, Austria-Hungary, and Italy are allied in the Triple Alliance. For one reason or another, Russia, Great Britain, and Serbia are on bad terms with one or more of the members of the Triple Alliance.

Now let's consider what the final sentence of the paragraph implies:

> **Because** France needed allies to oppose this formidable Triple Alliance. . . .

In light of the implications earlier in the paragraph, you might conclude that:

> France turned to Great Britain, Russia, or Serbia.

You would be correct. In fact, France turned to Russia and Great Britain, forming the Triple Entente with them, in opposition to the Triple Alliance. And what about Serbia? World War I began when Archduke Francis Ferdinand of Austria-Hungary was assassinated by a Serbian nationalist. That should not seem surprising if you read the paragraph carefully and think about all the implications of the statements in it.

From your work with this paragraph, you should see that it is important to consider all the implications of the statements in a piece of writing before you draw a conclusion. Keep an open mind; consider all the possibilities.

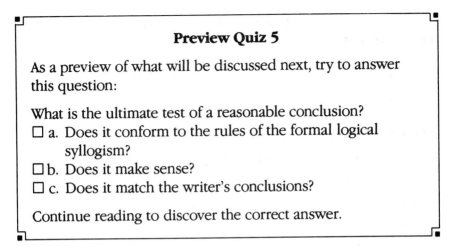

Preview Quiz 5

As a preview of what will be discussed next, try to answer this question:

What is the ultimate test of a reasonable conclusion?
☐ a. Does it conform to the rules of the formal logical syllogism?
☐ b. Does it make sense?
☐ c. Does it match the writer's conclusions?

Continue reading to discover the correct answer.

Sometimes it is necessary to draw a conclusion not from a direct statement in a piece of writing but from the unstated main idea of the writing. Consider the information in this paragraph:

> The cactus plant usually has a thick green trunk. This trunk performs the photosynthesis that, in other plants, is performed by leaves. Generally, cactus plants do not have leaves. The leaves of a tree expose an enormous surface area to the sun and wind. All over that surface area evaporation of water takes place all the time. The trunk of the cactus, in contrast, exposes a much smaller area, thereby reducing evaporation even in the harsh conditions of the desert.

The main idea of the paragraph is not stated, but it is easy to determine. It could be stated as:

> The cactus plant is well suited to its desert environment.

This fact has several implications that could lead to valid conclusions. You could conclude that if you intend to keep a cactus as a houseplant, you will have to try to duplicate its desert environment. You will have to keep it in a sunny spot, and you will have to be careful not to give it too much water. You can also conclude that, if you live in a desert area, you should forget about planting trees in your yard. From the information in the paragraph and the unstated main idea, you can conclude that trees are not well adapted to a desert environment. Water will evaporate from their leaves too quickly, and they will wither and die.

As you read, watch for potential causes. Think about their implications. Stretch your thinking; go beyond the obvious and try to imagine what all the implications of the statements may be. Remember that one cause may have many effects and one set of facts may lead to several conclusions. Avoid drawing a final conclusion until you are satisfied that you have explored all the avenues that the implications may lead you to. Then put the results of your thinking together. Evaluate it in light of what the writing says and what you know. Decide which outcomes seem most likely. Then draw your conclusions. Test them by deciding whether they make sense; remember that making sense is the ultimate test of any conclusion.

PART THREE

Sample Exercise

The exercise on the next page is a sample exercise. Its purpose is to show how the information you have studied in Parts One and Two can be put to use in reading.

A second purpose of the sample exercise is to preview the thirty exercises that appear in Part Four. Reading the sample passage and answering the sample questions will help you get off to a good start.

The answers to all the questions are fully explained. Reasons are given showing why the correct answers are the best answers and where the wrong answers are faulty. In addition, the text describes the thinking you might do as you work through the exercise correctly.

Complete the sample exercise carefully and thoughtfully. Do not go on to Part Four until you are certain that you understand what a conclusion is and how to draw accurate conclusions.

Sample Exercise

Picture yourself, if you will, having to deal with this problem. Rick Donner, a scuba diver, was diving alone in the Pacific off the California coast. His marker buoy, floating on the surface, carried the divers' flag to warn boats that there was a diver down. He had been swimming for an hour, enjoying the solitude among the thick graceful strands of an undersea kelp forest, checking his air supply every so often until, all too soon, it was time to surface. As Rick went up, a huge wave surged past overhead and rolled on toward the shore. At the same time, Rick felt himself jerked backward. The wave had dragged the anchor of his marker buoy, tangling its line around Rick's air hose and tearing it apart. Something had to be done, and quickly.

1. Because Rick was diving alone, you can conclude that
   ☐ a. no one was available to help him.
   ☐ b. the warning buoy did not work properly.
   ☐ c. he would have to surface sooner.
   ☐ d. someone else would soon be swimming by.

2. From the fact that the air hose was torn, you can conclude that
   ☐ a. another wave was on its way.
   ☐ b. air bubbles would alert rescuers.
   ☐ c. Rick's air supply would run out soon.
   ☐ d. Rick's diving partner would come to his aid.

3. From the main idea of the paragraph, you can conclude that a scuba diver
   ☐ a. does not require great strength.
   ☐ b. should never dive alone.
   ☐ c. should avoid swimming in kelp forests.
   ☐ d. should not buy used equipment.

4. Underline the sentence that supports the conclusion that boats will steer clear of the area where Rick is diving.

Answers and Explanations

1. To complete this sentence, you must decide what conclusion is implied by the fact that Rick was diving alone. Read each possible conclusion and decide whether it is implied by Rick's swimming alone.

   The best answer is *a.* You can verify this for yourself by thinking of a sentence that states the cause-and-effect relationship: *Because* Rick was diving alone, no one was available to help him.

   Answers *b* and *c* are incorrect because both state results that would not be caused by diving alone. The buoy would not be affected by the number of divers, nor would the length of time that Rick could stay below.

   Answer *d* is incorrect because it contradicts good sense. If someone is swimming alone, it is *unlikely* that someone else will soon be swimming by.

2. Again, completing this sentence requires you to find a conclusion implied by a cause. In this case the cause is the fact that the air hose was torn. In your mind, construct a sentence in which the cause begins with *because.* Then look for the best ending to it.

   The best answer is *c: Because* the air hose was torn, Rick's air supply would run out soon. This is a reasonable conclusion.

   Answer *a* is incorrect because the coming of another wave would not be affected by a torn air hose; there is no relationship between the two events.

   Answer *b* is incorrect because air bubbles could only alert rescuers if there were any nearby; we know from other evidence in the paragraph that there were none.

   Answer *d* is incorrect because we know that Rick was diving alone; he had no diving partner.

3. To complete this sentence, you must first decide what the main idea of the paragraph is. The story seems to lead to the idea that because of the possibility of the kind of trouble Rick got into, a diver should never dive alone.

The best answer is *b*.

Answer *a* is incorrect because nothing in the paragraph implies that strength is not needed. In fact, Rick might have been able to resist the force of the wave if he were stronger.

Answer *c* is incorrect because there is no relationship between Rick's swimming in the kelp forest and the wave; the wave caused the trouble, not the kelp.

Answer *d* is incorrect because it is not at all relevant to the facts in the paragraph. Nothing is mentioned about used equipment. Perhaps buying used equipment is not a good idea, but nothing in this paragraph leads to that conclusion.

4. When you are told to find a sentence that supports a certain conclusion, you are being told to find the cause of a certain effect. To do so, review the paragraph to find a likely cause, and then test it by adding the word *because* to it and seeing whether it implies the effect. The best answer is the sentence "His marker buoy, floating on the surface, carried the divers' flag to warn boats that there was a diver down." Try the test:

Because his marker buoy, floating on the surface, carried the divers' flag to warn boats that there was a diver down, boats would steer clear of the area.

If you had difficulty answering these questions correctly, review the paragraph and questions. If, after that, you still do not understand the answers and explanations, check with your instructor before going on.

PART FOUR

Practice Exercises

The thirty practice exercises that follow are designed to help you put to use your ability to understand conclusions and draw accurate conclusions.

Each exercise is just like the sample exercise you completed in Part Three.

Read each passage well and answer carefully and thoughtfully the four questions with it. Correct your answers, using the answer key at the back of the book. Record your progress on the chart on the inside back cover before going on to the next exercise.

· 1 ·

Before the development of modern printing methods, most paper was made of flax and hemp, the same fibers that were used to make cloth. When cheap, high-speed printing arrived, the demand for books skyrocketed. Paper manufacturers shifted from flax and hemp to wood, which was in much greater supply. Today, most paper is made from wood, and therein lies a problem. The most widely used method of turning wood into paper uses acids, and this produces paper high in acid content. Over the course of time, the acids react with air, moisture, and sunlight and make the paper brittle. It becomes so brittle that it cracks, crumbles, and even falls into dust. Paper with a high "rag content"—that is, paper made literally from rags or from fibers more like flax and hemp—is not subject to the same decaying process.

1. Because the demand for books suddenly increased when cheap, high-speed printing arrived, you can conclude that
   □ a. paper manufacturers were forced out of business.
   □ b. books had to be made to last longer.
   □ c. writers made much more money then than now.
   □ d. paper manufacturers had to increase production.

2. From the fact that paper made from wood becomes so brittle that it falls into dust, you can conclude that
   □ a. some books simply fall apart after a while.
   □ b. paper manufacturers are cheating the public.
   □ c. wood is dangerous as a building material.
   □ d. paper manufacturers had to increase production.

3. From the main idea of the paragraph, you can conclude that
   □ a. flax makes fine, durable fabrics for clothing.
   □ b. hemp makes flexible, durable rope.
   □ c. paper manufacturers use acids unnecessarily.
   □ d. many books may be in danger of falling apart.

4. Underline the sentence that supports the conclusion that paper with high rag content is best for long-lasting books.

· 2 ·

The male and female mosquito make an odd couple. The female is a vampire that lives on blood and may even need blood for the proper development of her eggs. The male is a vegetarian that sips nectar and plant juices. Females of different species choose different hosts on which to dine. Some feed exclusively on cattle, horses, birds, and other warm-blooded creatures. Some favor cold-blooded animals. Still others prefer human beings.

While the female's menu varies, her bite remains the same. She drives her sharp, tubular snout through the skin and injects a fluid to keep the blood from clotting. Then she drinks her fill of the freely flowing blood. The fluid that she injects may carry disease germs if she has previously bitten a diseased animal. After her blood meal, she rests while her eggs develop. She then looks for standing water in which to lay her eggs—a pond, a pool, a swamp, or even a pail of rainwater.

1. From information in the paragraphs, you can conclude that a mosquito that bites you at a picnic is
   □ a. male.
   □ b. diseased.
   □ c. female.
   □ d. resting.

2. From the fact that the fluid that a mosquito injects may carry disease germs you can conclude that mosquitoes
   □ a. are a health hazard to most living creatures.
   □ b. cannot be controlled effectively.
   □ c. render important services to humankind.
   □ d. are a necessary element in the balance of nature.

3. Because the injected fluid keeps blood from clotting,
   □ a. the victim may become diseased.
   □ b. the mosquito's eggs develop.
   □ c. the blood flows freely.
   □ d. it may contain germs.

4. Underline the sentence that implies that it would be wise to empty a wading pool in mosquito breeding season.

·3·

To be completely accurate, the word duck should be used only for the female members of the bird family Anatidae (UH-nad-uh-dee). The males are called drakes. However, in popular usage *duck* applies to the whole family. Ducks protect themselves from cold water by waterproofing themselves. Like most birds, ducks have glands that secrete oils. They use their bills to rub the waxy oil over their feathers. Under the oiled feathers is a layer of smaller, soft feathers called *down*. Down keeps ducks warm by trapping air under the outside feathers. Ducks that feed on the surface have light, hollow bones. Mergansers and other diving ducks have heavier bones than surface-feeding ducks. Diving ducks are excellent swimmers.

Most drakes are more brightly colored than female ducks. However, at the end of the mating season most ducks molt; that is, they lose their feathers. When they molt they are unable to fly. The drakes lose their brilliant plumage and turn a drabber but safer brown, like that of the females.

1. You can conclude that diving ducks are heavier than surface ducks because
   ☐ a. they eat more food.
   ☐ b. they survive only in cold climates.
   ☐ c. they do not lose their bright plumage after mating.
   ☐ d. their weight helps them stay underwater.

2. From the fact that the diving ducks are excellent underwater swimmers, you can conclude that
   ☐ a. other ducks cannot swim underwater.
   ☐ b. diving ducks are able to pursue fish underwater.
   ☐ c. diving ducks do not molt.
   ☐ d. diving ducks do not require protective coloration.

3. For a while after the mating season is over, drakes
   ☐ a. do not swim.
   ☐ b. are unable to secrete oils normally.
   ☐ c. are more vulnerable than usual.
   ☐ d. acquire bright, brilliantly colored plumage.

4. Underline the sentence that supports the conclusion in number 3.

·4·

One thing strikes a visitor at Walnut Hills Community Elementary School near Denver. The rooms are gigantic and *there aren't any desks.* But watch your step! Children are lying all over the floor, some reading by themselves, some doing worksheets in groups of twos and threes; others sit in small groups asking questions of an adult. It looks as if the children have rebelled, occupied the superintendent's office, and are running the school the way they would like. But the superintendent of the Cherry Creek School District knows the school is running just the way he likes it. Many of the children come to school early and leave late—by choice. Absences have been halved. What's more, the children are learning academic subjects far better than average. And they understand a lot more about themselves and others than most children do.

1. From the fact that many of the children choose to come to school early and leave late you can conclude that
   - ☐ a. they enjoy the atmosphere at Walnut Hills.
   - ☐ b. children are unpredictable.
   - ☐ c. educators at Walnut Hills are discouraged.
   - ☐ d. classrooms are poorly furnished.

2. From the fact that the children are learning academic subjects far better than average you can conclude that
   - ☐ a. the educators at Walnut Hills are discouraged.
   - ☐ b. the techniques described are educationally sound.
   - ☐ c. the superintendent is likely to be fired.
   - ☐ d. there is a serious lack of equipment in the district.

3. Educators at the Walnut Hills Community Elementary School are
   - ☐ a. misguided.
   - ☐ b. uninterested.
   - ☐ c. progressive.
   - ☐ d. traditional.

4. Underline the sentence that supports the conclusion that changes at Walnut Hills have improved attendance.

· 5 ·

Long before European explorers and colonists landed on North American shores, tribes of Indians named the land and its features. Many of the original Indian names are still in use. Indians named areas of land for the people who lived there, and they also named the mountains, rivers, and other natural landmarks. Indians are known for their love of nature and the poetic way they described it. Many Indian place names have an appealing sound and rhythm. Today more than half of the states in the United States have names that are either identical to or derived from Indian names. Many names were first given to rivers, and then later used to name a state. Explorers, colonists, pioneers, and settlers named some states in honor of kings, queens, and places in the Old World. Some names are so ancient that history cannot tell us when and how they originated.

1. From information in the passage you can conclude that
   ☐ a. European explorers were responsible for most of the place names we use today.
   ☐ b. America's history is confused.
   ☐ c. Indians resented foreigners.
   ☐ d. Indian place names have endured for centuries.

2. From the main idea of the paragraph, you can conclude that America has been
   ☐ a. marked by a variety of influences.
   ☐ b. abused by its early pioneers.
   ☐ c. preserved by the Indians.
   ☐ d. a haven for downtrodden people from many lands.

3. The names that Indians gave to natural landmarks were generally
   ☐ a. fictitious in origin.
   ☐ b. hotly debated.
   ☐ c. decided by colonists.
   ☐ d. inspired by nature.

4. Underline the sentence that supports the conclusion in number 1.

·6·

The dancers wear bright Western costumes that blend into swirls of color as they melt from one pattern into another. On stage, a gentleman taps his left boot and calls: "Do-si-do and then you promenade your partner as you go rollin', rollin', you're rollin' down the river. . . ."

You can picture this scene at a grange hall where farmers have gathered for their weekly hoedown. But today, this activity is equally at home in a San Carlos gymnasium or even the Oakland Auditorium. Square dancing has moved into the suburbs and cities. There are eight square dance clubs in San Francisco alone.

Surprisingly, this dance is of comparatively recent vintage. Although its roots go back to European folk dancing, the square dance as a uniquely American folk dance form didn't evolve until the last century.

1. The conclusion that square dancing was first developed in the United States is
   ☐ a. accurate.
   ☐ b. questionable.
   ☐ c. false.
   ☐ d. impossible to assess.

2. From the description in the paragraph, you can conclude that square dancers
   ☐ a. are moving to California in great numbers.
   ☐ b. are energetic and enjoy "looking the part."
   ☐ c. are mostly from Europe.
   ☐ d. sing along as they dance.

3. The main idea of the second paragraph supports the conclusion that
   ☐ a. square dancing is increasing in popularity.
   ☐ b. square dancing is exhausting.
   ☐ c. square dancing is best done in a grange hall.
   ☐ d. farmers make the best square dancers.

4. Underline the sentence that supports the correct answer to number 1.

In recent years, millions of Americans have embraced the bicycle as if it were a startling new invention. There are more than seventy million bikes in the United States today, more than two for every three automobiles. Of course, the bike has been around for more than 150 years, and this isn't America's first bicycle boom. A wave of bike enthusiasm swept the land in the late 1800s, and bicycle production hit two million units in 1897. Then, with the coming of the auto, bicycling declined, and for decades it remained popular only with children and a few adult faddists. Now, a national preoccupation with air pollution and physical fitness has brought the bike back to the forefront. In a recent year, more than eight million bikes were sold in the United States, and a third of them went to adults. The year before, only 15 percent of new bike sales were for adults.

1. From the fact that it has been around for 150 years, you can conclude that the bicycle is likely to
   ☐ a. be abandoned soon.
   ☐ b. disappear when a replacement for the car is found.
   ☐ c. endure through waves of enthusiasm and neglect.
   ☐ d. reach record sales in the coming year.

2. From the main idea of the paragraph, you can conclude that the bicycle is
   ☐ a. enjoying a strong revival.
   ☐ b. creating traffic problems.
   ☐ c. popular only with children.
   ☐ d. replacing the family car.

3. You can conclude that
   ☐ a. bicycle sales to adults are growing especially fast.
   ☐ b. more than ten million bikes will be sold next year.
   ☐ c. 40 percent of sales will be to adults next year.
   ☐ d. children are losing interest in bicycling.

4. Underline the two sentences that support the correct answer for number 3.

·8·

A quarter century ago: November 9, 1965. It was a pleasant day. The evening exodus from the hearts of the great cities had just begun, when, without warning, lights in office towers flickered out and died at 5:16 P.M. Thousands of feet above, astonished airline pilots saw Manhattan fade, then disappear. In eight minutes, a near total electrical eclipse had swept over an area slightly smaller than Great Britain but crowded with thirty million people. A massive power failure had torn the intricate electrical grid that served parts of eight states and sections of Ontario, Canada. The Great Blackout, as it came to be called, was the first dramatic warning that the relationship between energy supply and demand had reached a precarious balance.

1. From the fact that all electrical power was lost in the affected area, you can conclude that
   □ a. elevators stopped.
   □ b. traffic lights blinked out.
   □ c. subway trains ground to a halt.
   □ d. all of the above occurred.

2. Because an electrical failure could sweep through such a large area in eight minutes you can conclude that
   □ a. such a thing could never happen again.
   □ b. the distribution network was fragile.
   □ c. Great Britain is likely to suffer a similar outage since it is approximately the same size.
   □ d. high demand in Manhattan was the cause.

3. You can conclude that
   □ a. planes en route to Manhattan had to land elsewhere.
   □ b. people in Great Britain began to panic when they heard the news.
   □ c. Canadians later withdrew from the electrical grid.
   □ d. people in the area sold their homes and moved.

4. Underline the sentence that supports the conclusion in number 3.

Shy, wary, and seldom seen, perhaps no creature in nature has suffered so much as the wise, perceptive raven. It is a shiny black bird, a member of the crow family. Primarily a scavenger, it will, like the other members of the crow family, eat grain crops, eggs, and fledgling chicks. Its call is a harsh, croaking caw. It can be tamed and taught to perform complicated tricks, even to mimic human speech.

The raven has been the object of superstition for centuries. In the myths and folklore of many countries, the raven was a bird of evil. Even the mere sighting of a raven was believed an evil omen. If one alighted on a church or dwelling, it was taken as a certain sign of death or disaster. In certain areas of the United States, some people still believe that the raven is an evil omen.

1. Because the raven sometimes eats crops, eggs, and chicks, you can conclude that
   □ a. farmers are fond of the magnificent bird.
   □ b. farmers dislike the bird.
   □ c. eggs make a bird's coat shiny.
   □ d. it is an intelligent bird.

2. From the fact that the raven's call is a harsh, croaking caw, you can conclude that
   □ a. its call does not win it friends and admirers.
   □ b. many people love to listen to it sing.
   □ c. it is possessed by demons.
   □ d. it is a shy, cautious bird.

3. From the main idea, you can conclude that the
   □ a. raven is an evil bird.
   □ b. raven is a friend to farmers everywhere, celebrated in the folklore of many countries.
   □ c. raven is an endangered species.
   □ d. raven's appearance, call, and habits inspired superstitions about it.

4. Underline the sentence that supports the conclusion that the raven is an intelligent bird.

· 10 ·

Freeways and streets often begin their careers with extra-wide lines. But soon traffic becomes heavier, and pressure increases on highway officials to "do something" about the congestion. Adding new lanes will require heavy equipment to create a base for a new road, perhaps digging away a hillside, or widening a bridge. And, it will take time. Officials may compromise and add part of a lane to the shoulder, move the paint stripes over a few inches, and create four lanes where three had been. It requires no heavy equipment and it's quick. Unfortunately, narrow lanes mean less room for drivers to correct their mistakes or inattention, and less room for the swaying of a car in a crosswind. Two cars on narrow lanes may actually touch even though the tires will be within their respective lanes.

1. Because adding new lanes will require heavy equipment and a great deal of work, you can conclude that doing so is
   □ a. the best solution.
   □ b. the traditional solution.
   □ c. expensive.
   □ d. inexpensive.

2. Because moving paint stripes requires no heavy equipment, you can conclude that doing so is
   □ a. the best solution.
   □ b. the traditional solution.
   □ c. expensive.
   □ d. inexpensive.

3. From the main idea, you can conclude that increasing the capacity of a road by narrowing the lanes
   □ a. is a costly, difficult, and time-consuming process.
   □ b. leads to safer, less-congested roads.
   □ c. offers the best long-term solution to congestion.
   □ d. is quick and cheap but potentially dangerous.

4. Underline the sentences that allow you to conclude that narrow lanes increase the danger of sideswipe collisions.

· 11 ·

In San Francisco there is an elite group of workers who commute twelve miles to their jobs by motor launch, then sit in the roomy cabin of a beautiful two-masted schooner reading, playing chess, watching TV, eating, or sleeping, until it is time to go to the office. The office is the bridge of a ship—freighter, tanker, or liner—headed for the Golden Gate Bridge.

These people are "bar pilots." They are a salty group of mariners who know the underwater contours lying off the city of San Francisco as well as they know the seamed palms of their hands. To them is entrusted the mission of guiding millions of tons of shipping safely across the great submerged sandbar that forms a barrier across the entrance to San Francisco Bay.

1. From the information in the first paragraph, you can conclude that
   ☐ a. bar pilots are pampered.
   ☐ b. sandbars discourage shipping.
   ☐ c. many freighter captains are inexperienced.
   ☐ d. bar pilots must be highly competent.

2. From the information in the second paragraph, you can conclude that
   ☐ a. bar pilots are pampered.
   ☐ b. sandbars discourage shipping.
   ☐ c. many freighter captains are inexperienced.
   ☐ d. bar pilots must be highly competent.

3. As a result of the great submerged sandbar at the entrance to San Francisco Bay, the bay is
   ☐ a. closed to large vessels.
   ☐ b. an important shipping area.
   ☐ c. closed to small pleasure craft.
   ☐ d. difficult to enter.

4. Underline the sentence that supports the conclusion that the bar pilots have studied the great sandbar thoroughly.

· 12 ·

The boomerang is two to four feet long (about half a meter to a meter), flat on one side, and rounded on the other. The smaller ones are really toys—the well-known "return" boomerangs. The thrower holds the boomerang vertically to throw it, but it tilts as it travels until it is in a horizontal attitude, with the curved side up. Air moving over the curved top side creates lift, as it does on an airplane wing. The boomerang whirls around in a curve and returns to the thrower. Anyone who has tried to throw a boomerang knows that it doesn't always return. That is the point of the hunting boomerang. It speeds toward its target with an irregular wobbling motion. A skilled hunter can bring down an animal at a distance as great as 400 feet, or more than 120 meters. The native people of Australia still use the boomerang for hunting.

1. Because air moving over the curved top side of a "return" boomerang creates lift, as it does on an airplane wing, the boomerang
   □ a. travels in a straight line.
   □ b. rises as it moves forward.
   □ c. drops to the ground.
   □ d. is still used in Australia.

2. Because the hunting boomerang speeds toward its target with an irregular wobbling motion, it
   □ a. is difficult to dodge.
   □ b. will return to the thrower.
   □ c. is easy to throw.
   □ d. is not very effective.

3. From the fact that the native people of Australia still use the boomerang for hunting, you can conclude that
   □ a. it is no longer used for sport.
   □ b. it remains an effective tool.
   □ c. game is plentiful in Australia.
   □ d. few people can throw a boomerang properly.

4. Underline the sentence that implies that the boomerang is not effective beyond 400 feet (120 meters).

· 13 ·

Most of us are reluctant to accept the fact that our natural resources are fixed—have been fixed, in fact, since the Earth was created. We want to go on using virgin materials. We aren't educated to reusing resources, or even recognizing the value of "waste" products. Currently, we are fearful of losing the use of our water and air to pollution. Perhaps, in the end, this fear may prove to be a good thing. We once thought of water and air as free, but they are not, not any more than the land is free. People haven't wanted to be educated about the part they must play in solving our environmental problems.

1. The main idea leads to the conclusion that
   - ☐ a. our attitudes lead to waste and pollution.
   - ☐ b. virgin materials are superior to recycled products.
   - ☐ c. we must adjust to shortages and high prices.
   - ☐ d. we can clean up our rivers and lakes.

2. Which sentence states the reasoning that led the writer to conclude that "this fear may prove to be a good thing"?
   - ☐ a. Because we fear air and water pollution, we will lapse into an era of pessimism and decay.
   - ☐ b. Because we fear air and water pollution, we will change our thinking about reusing resources.
   - ☐ c. Because we fear government controls, we will find better ways to dispose of waste.
   - ☐ d. Because we fear recycled materials, we will find new ways to exploit dwindling resources.

3. If it is true that, as a group, "we want to go on using virgin resources," then we will
   - ☐ a. enact legislation to that effect.
   - ☐ b. eliminate pollution by using them.
   - ☐ c. eliminate the fear we now feel.
   - ☐ d. exhaust a fixed supply of resources.

4. Underline the sentence that supports the conclusion that we now discard products that are potentially useful.

· 14 ·

All the guns around me now are in the hands of prison guards, but for fifteen years the guns were in my hands. Guns were my life, and your pharmacy was my business. I was a professional bandit, and among the places I robbed over the years I can count more than forty drugstores.

Why did I choose drugstores over other targets? I'll tell you, and I hope it will serve as a warning to the people who own and operate them. Most druggists simply don't believe holdups are ever going to happen to them. Most drugstores are located in areas where pedestrian traffic is heavy. There are narcotics on the premises. Pharmacies, moreover, are seldom heavily staffed.

1. Because most druggists don't believe that they will be held up, you can conclude that they
   □ a. take steps to protect their stores.
   □ b. are lax about security.
   □ c. close in the evening.
   □ d. demand police protection.

2. Because most drugstores are located in areas where pedestrian traffic is heavy,
   □ a. a thief can get "lost in the crowd."
   □ b. they are not attractive targets for thieves.
   □ c. they are difficult to find.
   □ d. they go unnoticed by the police.

3. Because narcotics are kept on the premises in drugstores, you can conclude that
   □ a. most people avoid entering drugstores.
   □ b. police avoid patrolling near drugstores.
   □ c. thieves do not consider drugstores worth robbing.
   □ d. thieves who are addicts are attracted to drugstores.

4. Underline the sentence that allows you to conclude that a thief usually finds little opposition in a drugstore.

· 15 ·

A purebred dog is a type of dog that is recognized by the American Kennel Club as a distinct breed. When they are mature, purebred dogs of the same breed vary little in size, weight, and other physical traits. In addition, dogs of a particular breed usually have definite temperament and behavior characteristics.

On the other hand, mongrels, or dogs of mixed breeds, vary widely and unpredictably. The cute, cuddly, mongrel puppy that you select at random may grow into a big, long-haired, pony-sized animal instead of the small pet you really wanted. The long-legged mongrel puppy that you visualize as a large-sized companion for country walks may stop growing soon and turn out to be a small house-loving pet.

1. From the information in the first paragraph, you can conclude that if you buy a purebred puppy
   - ☐ a. it will be of moderate size when it is grown.
   - ☐ b. it will be more attractive than a mongrel dog.
   - ☐ c. you can predict its characteristics when it is grown.
   - ☐ d. you will have a large-sized companion for country walks.

2. From the information in the second paragraph, you can conclude that if you buy a mongrel puppy
   - ☐ a. it will be of moderate size when it is grown.
   - ☐ b. it will be more attractive than a purebred dog.
   - ☐ c. you cannot predict its characteristics when it is grown.
   - ☐ d. you will have a large-sized companion for country walks.

3. From the main idea, you can conclude that the greatest advantage in choosing a purebred puppy is that it is
   - ☐ a. predictable.
   - ☐ b. adaptable.
   - ☐ c. superior.
   - ☐ d. inferior.

4. Underline the sentence that supports the conclusion that purebred dogs enjoy a definite status.

· 16 ·

Not long ago, Les Halles—the teeming, crowded central food market that Emile Zola called "the belly of Paris"—was moved to a new site south of the city, near Orly Airport. The French mourned the end of an era. Paris is not a city accustomed to sudden change, and Les Halles represented a tradition going back to medieval times. An open-air market was established at the site of Les Halles Centrales some nine hundred years ago. In the mid-nineteenth century, Napoleon III commissioned architect Victor Baltard to design buildings to enclose the sprawling market. Baltard's twelve enormous iron and glass pavilions were acclaimed as architectural masterworks, but visitors were even more intrigued by the rich carnival of life that swirled around them. In recent times, however, it became apparent that Les Halles was not up to the task of feeding a growing city.

1. Which statement supports the conclusion that Les Halles was a traditional fixture of Parisian life?
   ☐ a. Les Halles was moved to a new site.
   ☐ b. A rich carnival of life swirled around visitors.
   ☐ c. The market was established nine hundred years ago.
   ☐ d. The pavilions were architectural masterworks.

2. Which statement supports the conclusion that Parisians appreciate tradition?
   ☐ a. Les Halles was moved to a new site.
   ☐ b. Paris is not a city accustomed to sudden change.
   ☐ c. The pavilions were architectural masterworks.
   ☐ d. Les Halles was not up to feeding a growing city.

3. Which statement supports the conclusion that Les Halles was a lively, bustling place?
   ☐ a. A rich carnival of life swirled around visitors.
   ☐ b. Paris is not a city accustomed to sudden change.
   ☐ c. The market was established nine hundred years ago.
   ☐ d. The pavilions were architectural masterworks.

4. Underline the sentence that supports the conclusion that a new market was necessary.

35

· 17 ·

Most of the huge presses that are used to make objects from sheets of metal are driven by hydraulic pressure, and therefore they are called hydraulic presses. Basically, a hydraulic press has three parts: a small cylinder with a small piston inside it, a large cylinder with a large piston inside it, and a pipe that connects the two cylinders. The whole device is filled with fluid. When a force is applied to the small piston, the fluid transmits the force to the large piston. The small piston is pushed with a small force through a long distance, and the large piston moves through a short distance with a much greater force. This large piston presses the sheet of metal against the die that shapes it.

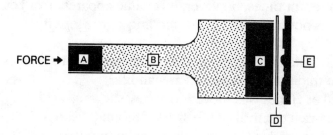

1. From the information in the passage, you can conclude that part A in the diagram is the
   - ☐ a. fluid.
   - ☐ b. small piston.
   - ☐ c. large cylinder.
   - ☐ d. sheet metal.

2. From the information in the passage, you can conclude that part B in the diagram is the
   - ☐ a. die.
   - ☐ b. large piston.
   - ☐ c. small piston.
   - ☐ d. fluid.

3. From the information in the passage, you can conclude that part D in the diagram is the
   - ☐ a. die.
   - ☐ b. small piston.
   - ☐ c. large piston.
   - ☐ d. sheet metal.

4. Underline the sentence that allows you to reach a conclusion about the part labeled E in the diagram.

· 18 ·

In recent years, there has been much public discussion about techniques designed to help people increase their reading speed. So much depends on definition. Among the general public there is some disagreement about exactly what we mean when we speak of "reading" a page of print. For some people, it is attention to and interpretation of most of the words on the page. Others seem to mean simply "dealing with large groups of words by speeding through them and picking out highlights." However, most reading experts stress the importance of increasing the level of *comprehension*—the level of true understanding of words and the ideas they stand for. They believe that there has been over-emphasis on the "numbers game" of increasing the number of words a person can "run through" per minute.

1. The reader may conclude from the paragraph that
   □ a. rapid reading improves reading comprehension.
   □ b. rapid reading is useless.
   □ c. comprehension is more important than speed.
   □ d. reading professionals ignore students' needs.

2. You can conclude that most reading experts would think that a person who reads slowly with high comprehension
   □ a. should use techniques to increase reading speed.
   □ b. is reading well.
   □ c. would make a good subject for research.
   □ d. should concentrate more on understanding individual words.

3. Which of the following conclusions can be drawn from the main idea of the paragraph?
   □ a. Reading is a simple intellectual activity.
   □ b. Rapid reading guarantees comprehension.
   □ c. Reading specialists should compromise.
   □ d. Reading requires many skills.

4. Underline the sentence that implies that the public is interested in techniques to increase reading speed.

· 19 ·

How do you reach and inspire youngsters who have turned off and given up on furthering their education? How do you bring them in off the streets of Harlem and convince them that regular attendance at high school courses will eventually provide them with the tools for success? Edward F. Carpenter, headmaster of "The Prep," as it is known by the students, admits that it isn't easy. "We reach these young people with the concept of school as a place where they will find respect, belief in their abilities, and an attitude of sincerely caring about their problems," Carpenter states. "Our purpose is to build within each student an awareness of his worth and capabilities and to persuade him that there is a group of adults as well as members of his own peer group who will pull with him."

1. From the statements that headmaster Carpenter makes, you can conclude that "The Prep" works at
   ☐ a. improving the self-image of young people.
   ☐ b. protecting youthful offenders from prosecution.
   ☐ c. maintaining law and order in the streets.
   ☐ d. transforming athletes into students.

2. You can conclude that headmaster Carpenter
   ☐ a. teaches English.
   ☐ b. considers traditional academic subjects of primary importance.
   ☐ c. considers attitudes as important as academics.
   ☐ d. uses sports to build character.

3. You can conclude that headmaster Carpenter thinks "turned-off" youngsters respond to
   ☐ a. traditional education.
   ☐ b. formal discipline.
   ☐ c. financial incentive.
   ☐ d. individualized attention.

4. Underline the sentence that supports the conclusion that headmaster Carpenter does not have any illusions about the difficulty of his job.

· 20 ·

In the minds of many Americans, Boston is a kind of historic blur, a vast urban museum of old monuments, baked bean factories, and people named Lowell and Cabot who talk only to each other and to God. The musty aura of Boston's image may linger in part because the city itself doesn't boast of being the biggest or boomingest of places, nor does it aspire to such goals. In its own low-key self-promotion, Boston neither brags of its past nor projects some galactic future. Boston prides itself on being *livable*. It is not just old monuments or just contemporary dazzle, but a growing variety of attractions that has made Boston seem so livable. This perception of the city is so widespread that, a few years ago, in a survey of Ivy League graduates, Boston replaced New York as the city most favored as a place to live and work after college.

1. The paragraph supports the conclusion that a livable city
   - ☐ a. is brassy and booming.
   - ☐ b. projects a galactic future.
   - ☐ c. avoids extremes.
   - ☐ d. follows tradition.

2. From the description in the paragraph, you can conclude that the people of Boston
   - ☐ a. have a sense of history and a view of the future.
   - ☐ b. are self-centered and ignore the rest of the country.
   - ☐ c. are dull and old-fashioned.
   - ☐ d. have no drive and ambition.

3. If Boston is a kind of historic blur in the minds of many Americans, then they are
   - ☐ a. correct.
   - ☐ b. incorrect.
   - ☐ c. interested in history.
   - ☐ d. Ivy League graduates.

4. Underline the sentence that supports the conclusion in number 1.

· 21 ·

"Buckle up . . . or else!" may become the slogan of those who support safety belts. Studies have shown that most injuries and deaths resulting from accidents are caused when people are thrown out of or against the interior of the vehicle. Forty percent of those killed in auto accidents would have been saved if they had been wearing safety belts. Safety belts have been standard equipment on all automobiles sold in the United States for twenty-five years. Since long before that, safety-minded organizations have been advocating that motor vehicle drivers and passengers make it a habit to use safety belts whether they are driving across the country or across town. Millions of dollars worth of public service advertising has been donated by newspapers, magazines, radio, and television to remind motorists and passengers to "buckle up."

1. Since most injuries are caused by being thrown out of or against the interior of the vehicle, you can conclude that
   ☐ a. people are better off if they can leap out of a car.
   ☐ b. people are better off if they are strapped in place.
   ☐ c. safety belts themselves must be causing injuries.
   ☐ d. most people must be using safety belts.

2. Because 40 percent of those killed in auto accidents were not wearing safety belts, you can conclude that
   ☐ a. nearly everyone wears safety belts now.
   ☐ b. only careless drivers do not wear safety belts.
   ☐ c. the cost of installing safety belts has been wasted.
   ☐ d. many people do not wear safety belts.

3. The campaign for safety belts is supported by
   ☐ a. insurance companies only.
   ☐ b. all licensed motorists.
   ☐ c. safety organizations only.
   ☐ d. safety organizations and the media.

4. Underline the sentence that supports the conclusion that the lifesaving value of safety belts has been established.

·22·

Coleridge's "Ancient Mariner," becalmed upon a glassy ocean and dying of thirst, was not the only one to be surrounded by water he dared not drink. Our rivers and lakes are in serious trouble as they continue to bear never-intended burdens of pollution and industrial expansion. Our waters are not fit to drink unless they are first treated or purified. At a treatment station, water may pass through several processes. Filtration is the simplest and most obvious of these; the water is passed through filters, which may be fine or coarse, depending on how the water will be used. Next, the water may be aerated—sprayed into the air to release gases dissolved in it. Bacteria in water can be eliminated by adding chlorine, bubbling ozone through the water, or by exposing the water to ultraviolet light. All of these treatment methods are expensive. Treating our waste water *before* it is discharged into lakes, rivers, or the ocean is far less expensive.

1. You can conclude that filtration removes
   □ a. gases.
   □ b. bacteria.
   □ c. dirt.
   □ d. ozone.

2. You can conclude that at a treatment station what looks like a fountain is
   □ a. an aeration device.
   □ b. a monument to Coleridge.
   □ c. intended to heighten community awareness.
   □ d. meant to emphasize recreational uses of water.

3. It is logical to conclude that chlorine, ozone, and ultraviolet light
   □ a. are cheap methods of treating water.
   □ b. release gases trapped in water.
   □ c. are troublesome pollutants in water.
   □ d. will kill bacteria.

4. Underline the sentence that supports the conclusion that sewage treatment is the first step in water treatment.

· 23 ·

Although commonly thought to be one of humankind's feared deep-sea enemies, the octopus is generally a harmless animal that rarely bothers people. In fact, most types of this powerful, eight-armed creature are afraid of people. There have been some cases in which octopuses have attacked divers, but even these scattered attacks have not been very serious. In the mid-nineteenth century, Victor Hugo is said to have started the idea that the octopus is a vicious monster of the deep. In his novel *Toilers of the Sea*, he described a devilfish eating a human being. The tale became so popular that other novelists, and later the movies, used episodes that depicted a person struggling in the arms of this marine monster. Thus, the misconception of the octopus as a vicious, merciless killer was spread.

1. The reader can conclude that
   ☐ a. the octopus is defenseless.
   ☐ b. Victor Hugo was a popular novelist.
   ☐ c. Victor Hugo was a marine biologist.
   ☐ d. every octopus is friendly.

2. The paragraph implies that novelists
   ☐ a. deal only with facts.
   ☐ b. sometimes choose topics to appeal to popular fancy.
   ☐ c. always intentionally distort the truth.
   ☐ d. often fail to win critical acclaim.

3. The author implies that
   ☐ a. deep-sea diving is dangerous.
   ☐ b. most sea creatures are harmless.
   ☐ c. stories of the octopus have been exaggerated.
   ☐ d. sea stories have always enjoyed widespread popularity.

4. Underline the sentence that suggests that writers borrow ideas from one another.

·24·

A tunnel may be used for moving people, freight, or water, or to hold utility lines. Most tunnels are used in mining. Mining techniques are special, however, and rarely resemble "true" tunneling. The next most common use for tunnels is to move water (including moving it out of mines). Water-supply tunnels were built in the ancient world, sometimes over considerable distances. One water-supply tunnel, explored by modern archaeologists, was driven 3,000 feet (more than 900 meters) through the base of a hill on the Greek island of Samos in the sixth century B.C. Herodotus, the Greek historian, thought the Samos tunnel was one of the greatest engineering feats of his time. Considering the crude equipment the tunnelers had to work with, it was. However, the Greek tunnelers failed to meet in the middle. The two tunneling gangs missed each other under the hill and had to engineer a double hairpin turn to finish the job.

1. It can be concluded that tunnels are
   ☐ a. nearly obsolete in the modern world.
   ☐ b. an ancient engineering feat.
   ☐ c. a relatively recent modern development.
   ☐ d. an expensive way to transport goods.

2. Because of their crude equipment, the Greek tunnelers
   ☐ a. failed to meet in the middle.
   ☐ b. could not agree on important details.
   ☐ c. failed to take the time they needed.
   ☐ d. could not follow the advice of Herodotus.

3. You can conclude that tunnels
   ☐ a. jeopardize the balance of nature.
   ☐ b. can be at least as long as 3,000 feet (900 meters).
   ☐ c. can be used for human habitation.
   ☐ d. contribute to the beautification of the landscape.

4. Underline the sentence that supports the conclusion that maintaining a steady supply of water was a key concern on the island of Samos in the sixth century B. C.

· 25 ·

The magic spades of archaeology have given us the whole lost world of Egypt. Thanks to the Egyptian climate, we know more about the vanished Egyptians than we know about any other ancient people, much more than we know about the early Greeks and Romans, whose civilizations died just yesterday. The climate in Egypt is extremely dry. Almost nothing rots, spoils, or crumbles away. Dig up the most delicate carving, the finest substance, and you will find it as fresh and perfect after thousands of years of lying in the sand as if it had recently come from the artist's hand. The Egyptians often buried useful objects with their dead. When they didn't bury the actual objects, they buried little models of them, exact reproductions of the real things. Is it any wonder that we have a complete record of their civilization?

1. Because the climate in Egypt is extremely dry,
   ☐ a. ancient civilizations are not buried very deep.
   ☐ b. archaeologists must use advanced digging methods.
   ☐ c. almost nothing rots, spoils, or crumbles away.
   ☐ d. the Egyptians had to use secret methods of preservation.

2. From the fact that Egyptians often buried useful objects with their dead, you can conclude that the Egyptians
   ☐ a. were advanced in the arts.
   ☐ b. thought the dead needed these things.
   ☐ c. had no respect for their dead.
   ☐ d. were interested in archaeology.

3. Because the Egyptians buried useful objects or models of them with their dead,
   ☐ a. archaeology is more widely respected.
   ☐ b. we know what objects the Egyptians used.
   ☐ c. Egyptian civilization was a model for the Greeks.
   ☐ d. they have crumbled to dust.

4. Underline the sentence that supports the conclusion that the climate in Greece and Rome does not preserve artifacts as well as the Egyptian climate does.

Scientists are studying causes and cures for the peculiar malady known as "jet lag." Our bodies are programmed for rhythmic changes during each twenty-four-hour period called the "circadian cycle," generating more energy during busy daytime hours, less at night, and so on. When we hop a jet and fly through six time zones, our system gets confused. Energy signals are issued at the wrong times, and we may spend the first days of that dream vacation feeling exhausted because our bodies don't know what time it is. You can lessen the shock of change by following these steps:

- Start adjusting to your new time schedule a few days before beginning your trip.
- Get as much sleep as possible en route to your destination.
- Break long trips with stopovers.
- Upon arrival, take it easy. Don't try to adjust to local time schedules all at once.

1. If you start adjusting to your new time schedule a few days before beginning your trip, then you will
   □ a. have a smaller adjustment to make on arrival.
   □ b. be exhausted by the time you arrive.
   □ c. cross fewer time zones during your trip.
   □ d. better understand the "circadian cycle."

2. If you get as much sleep as possible en route to your destination, then you will
   □ a. trick your body into thinking that it is at home.
   □ b. substitute "jet lag" for "circadian cycle."
   □ c. be rested when you arrive.
   □ d. not know the local time when you arrive.

3. If you break long trips with stopovers, you give your body time to
   □ a. cycle.   □ c. lag.
   □ b. adjust.   □ d. work.

4. Underline the sentences that imply that you should not plan much activity on your first day at your destination.

· 27 ·

Hunters may shoot their prey from quite a distance, but photographers find that the atmosphere deteriorates the image too much beyond a hundred yards—ninety meters or so. With a gun you need only put a single shot into your victim, but with a movie camera you may need four hundred pictures smoothly joined by a movement so perfect that those pictures will not jiggle or jump when they are projected—and every picture must be in sharp focus!

I think every nature photographer believes that some personal demon follows him or her about with the sole purpose of thwarting his or her every effort. When the sun is shining everything is quiet, but the moment it disappears behind a cloud the action starts. Put a big telephoto lens on your camera and an alligator catches a fish right under your nose.

1. From the main idea of the first paragraph, you can conclude that the author considers nature photography
   ☐ a. more difficult than hunting.
   ☐ b. financially rewarding.
   ☐ c. a profession haunted by demons and gremlins.
   ☐ d. always amusing.

2. Because the atmosphere deteriorates the image too much beyond a hundred yards, the photographer
   ☐ a. must get closer to the subject.
   ☐ b. needs a variety of expensive equipment.
   ☐ c. requires a sunny, unclouded sky.
   ☐ d. must use a large telephoto lens.

3. Because moving cameras must not jiggle or jump, you can conclude that the nature cinematographer must have
   ☐ a. a sharp eye.
   ☐ b. the largest telephoto lens.
   ☐ c. a vivid imagination.
   ☐ d. a steady hand.

4. Underline the sentence that suggests that it would be a good idea for a nature photographer to carry two cameras with lenses for closeups and distant shots.

· 28 ·

The scorpion is a fierce-looking creature with an armored, jointed body supported by eight legs. It has many eyes, yet for all practical purposes, it is almost blind. It feels its way around with large, fingerlike pincers. These pincers are powerful weapons with which the scorpion seizes and crushes its prey. The jointed tail, with its poisonous needle point, can be used with deadly accuracy in case the pincers are not effective. Sinister as they may be in the insect world, scorpions devour many varieties of insects that destroy grain fields. In one day, for example, an adult scorpion dines on nearly a hundred of these destructive insects. Though a person will find the pain from a scorpion's sting sharp, and the pain may last a few days, there is little danger of serious or lasting damage.

1. The author implies that people
   - ☐ a. need not fear scorpions.
   - ☐ b. should breed scorpions for crop protection.
   - ☐ c. should kill scorpions outside grain fields.
   - ☐ d. should consider keeping scorpions as pets.

2. You can conclude that, because the scorpion is almost blind, it
   - ☐ a. is not aware of prey at a distance.
   - ☐ b. moves with amazing speed.
   - ☐ c. lashes out viciously with its needle-sharp tail.
   - ☐ d. can inflict terrible damage on human beings.

3. The paragraph implies that the scorpion uses its poison
   - ☐ a. whenever it is threatened.
   - ☐ b. as a last resort.
   - ☐ c. to provoke its enemies.
   - ☐ d. only against people.

4. Underline the sentence that suggests that scorpions are useful to farmers.

The image of the forester as a rugged woodsman riding guard on national forests is not an accurate picture today. Although outdoor work is still important, forestry today requires management, mathematics, engineering, and human relations skills as well as professional forestry competence. At one time or another, a forester may specialize in timber management, range management, soil conservation, watershed protection, wildlife, forest recreation, fire control, and many similar tasks. A forester must help the nation meet its needs for forest products and uses, while at the same time ensuring, through multiple-use and sustained-yield programs, that these products and uses will be available in the future.

1. Which of the following conclusions is justified?
   - ☐ a. National forests are maintained at great expense to the taxpayer.
   - ☐ b. Foresters play a minor role in the preservation of national forests.
   - ☐ c. The United States is rapidly exhausting its natural resources.
   - ☐ d. Foresters require broad education and training to meet the demands of the job.

2. You can conclude that the most important quality in a prospective forester is
   - ☐ a. brute strength and daring.
   - ☐ b. flexibility and intelligence.
   - ☐ c. political connections.
   - ☐ d. practical "horse sense."

3. Foresters make an important contribution to
   - ☐ a. national security.
   - ☐ b. ecology and conservation.
   - ☐ c. political stability.
   - ☐ d. world trade.

4. Underline the sentences that allow you to conclude that the role of foresters has changed in recent times.

· 30 ·

The nation's twenty-seven thousand active veterinarians work in thirty fields of interest. The major areas are public health, research, and private practice. Most veterinarians are in private practice treating livestock and pets. Many work for federal, state, and local governments, inspecting food, enforcing health laws, and combating environmental problems. Some serve in the armed forces, caring for sentry dogs, maintaining base sanitation, and carrying out other disease-prevention activities. Some are teachers and researchers. And some work in industry helping to develop new drugs and foods.

Once concerned solely with livestock in rural areas, veterinary medicine has evolved into a complex and varied profession. Today's veterinarians, mostly city-based, not only deal with a broad range of animal diseases but also play a widening role in improving conditions for human health.

1. You can conclude that the role of veterinarians is
   - ☐ a. expanding to meet the needs of the times.
   - ☐ b. limited to treating livestock and pets.
   - ☐ c. aimed at serving rural communities.
   - ☐ d. limited to combating environmental problems.

2. Modern veterinarians must
   - ☐ a. travel extensively.
   - ☐ b. work for government agencies.
   - ☐ c. be knowledgeable in many areas.
   - ☐ d. practice in cities.

3. The science of veterinary medicine has
   - ☐ a. stood still.
   - ☐ b. been replaced.
   - ☐ c. changed dramatically.
   - ☐ d. all but disappeared.

4. Underline the sentence that supports the conclusion that a small percentage of today's veterinarians live in rural areas.

PART FIVE

Writing Activities

The writing activities that follow will help you draw conclusions in writing. They will also help you apply that skill to your own writing.

Complete each activity carefully. Your teacher may ask you to work alone or may prefer to have you work with other students. In many cases, you will be asked to write your answers on separate paper. Your teacher may ask you to write those answers in a notebook or journal so that all your writing activities will be in the same place. Because the activities gradually increase in difficulty, you should review each completed activity before you begin a new one. Reread the lesson in Parts One and Two (pages 5–14) if you have any questions about drawing conclusions.

▪ *Writing Activity 1* ▪

Read the following passage from "He" by Katherine Anne Porter.

> Life was very hard for the Whipples. It was hard to feed all the hungry mouths, it was hard to keep the children in flannels during the winter, short as it was: "God knows what would become of us if we lived North," they would say: keeping them decently clean was hard. "It looks like our luck won't never let up on us," said Mr. Whipple, but Mrs. Whipple was all for taking what was sent and calling it good, anyhow when the neighbors were in earshot. "Don't ever let a soul hear us complain," she kept saying to her husband. She couldn't stand to be pitied.

A. Complete each sentence by drawing a logical conclusion. Your teacher may ask you to discuss your answers with the class.

1. You can conclude that the Whipples live in a particular part of the United States. What part do you think they live in?

    _____

    _____

2. Mr. Whipple says, "It looks like our luck won't never let up on us," when talking about what the family has been through. You can conclude that the family _____

    _____

    _____

3. Mrs. Whipple says she does not want the neighbors to pity her. You can conclude that she _____

    _____

    _____

B. On a separate piece of paper or in your writing notebook, answer the following questions. Your teacher may ask you to work together with another student. Remember to refer back to the details in the passage when answering the questions.

1. Why do you think the Whipple family has struggled in life?

2. Who seems to be stronger, Mr. Whipple or Mrs. Whipple? What does the character say to support your conclusion?

3. The neighbors probably donate food and clothing to help the Whipples. Do the Whipples appreciate the neighbors' generosity? Do you think the neighbors look down on the Whipples? What details support your conclusion?

▪ *Writing Activity 2* ▪

Read the following passage from "The Prince" by Craig Nova. The neatly dressed prince is watching from under a tent as people arrive for the auction at his home.

> A young lawyer, a man who represented creditors, had come to the prince a month before the sale, offering to arrange with Christie's or Parke-Bernet and some private collectors a sale of some of the more interesting things. The prince thanked him for his consideration, and told him that all would be welcome at the sale. The young lawyer blushed when he left, not entirely certain himself whether because he saw that his suit was a cheaper imitation of the prince's or because he'd been shown what vile [bad, evil] stuff money was. As far as the prince was concerned, that vileness would be shared by all, or at least witnessed by all. Until this point the young lawyer had thought the finest thing was to be rich. . . .

A. Think about the young lawyer. What conclusions can you draw about him? What does he look like? Is he self-confident? Why do you think the lawyer blushes after talking to the prince?

   On a separate piece of paper or in your writing notebook, make a list of your ideas. Then write a short paragraph that includes some of the conclusions you have drawn about the young lawyer. Use your list of ideas to help you.

B. Think about the prince in the passage. What conclusions can you draw about him? Is he young or old? Why are his possessions up for sale? Is he ashamed to be losing his possessions? What does the young lawyer think of him?

   On a separate piece of paper or in your writing notebook, make a list of your ideas. Then write a short paragraph using some of the conclusions you have drawn about the prince. Use your list of ideas to help you.

▪ *Writing Activity 3* ▪

Read the following passage from *Women of Courage* by Margaret Truman. Susan B. Anthony was a crusader for woman's rights during the 1850s.

> In 1852 Susan B. Anthony attended a rally in Albany where she was refused permission to speak because of her sex. The incident made her so angry that she withdrew from the regular temperance organization [a group that wanted to ban alcoholic beverages] and set up a separate Woman's New York State Temperance Society with Elizabeth Cady Stanton as its president.
>
> Not long after that, Susan went to a convention of the New York State Teacher's Association. More than two-thirds of the members were women, but the men ran the entire meeting, giving the speeches, voting on resolutions, and generally ignoring the women, who sat in an isolated bloc at the back of the room.

A. On a separate piece of paper or in your writing notebook, answer the following questions. Refer back to the passage to check your answers. Your teacher may ask you to discuss your answers with the class.

1. Think about the cause-and-effect relationships you learned about in Part Two (pages 7–12). Remember that certain causes imply certain effects. When drawing a conclusion, decide which statements imply certain results. What conclusions can you draw from the passage above? What kind of person was Susan B. Anthony? What statements led you to your conclusions?

2. Imagine that you had attended the conference with Susan B. Anthony. What do you think she said to the men?

B. Choose a person you know or have read about who showed courage in a particular situation. On a separate piece of paper or in your writing notebook, list some qualities that describe the person. What is he or she like? Do you respect the person? What reason (or cause) led him or her to be courageous? What happened as a result of that cause?

Write a brief paragraph describing the courageous person. Use your list of ideas to help you. After you have finished your paragraph, ask another student to read it. What conclusions can the student draw about the person in your paragraph?

▪ *Writing Activity 4* ▪

A. Carla heard the hurricane warning sirens. Her youngest son, Louis, was due home twenty minutes ago.

On a separate piece of paper or in your writing notebook, describe what happens to Carla and Louis. If Carla hears hurricane warning sirens, where does she live? Why is Louis late? What can you conclude about Carla's feelings? Your paragraph should lead a reader to a reasonable conclusion.

B. Ask another student to read your paragraph and have him or her draw a conclusion. Do you agree with the conclusion? Is the conclusion logical? What in your writing helped the student to draw that conclusion? Your teacher may want you to share the results with the class.

ANSWER KEY

Practice Exercise 1
1. d   2. a   3. d
4. Paper with a high "rag content"—that is, paper made literally from rags or from fibers more like flax and hemp—is not subject to the same decaying process.

Practice Exercise 2
1. c   2. a   3. c
4. She then looks for standing water in which to lay her eggs—a pond, a pool, a swamp, or even a pail of rainwater.

Practice Exercise 3
1. d   2. b   3. c
4. When they molt they are unable to fly.

Practice Exercise 4
1. a   2. b   3. c
4. Absences have been halved.

Practice Exercise 5
1. d   2. a   3. d
4. Many of the original Indian names are still in use.

Practice Exercise 6
1. a   2. b   3. a
4. Although its roots go back to European folk dancing, the square dance as a uniquely American folk dance form didn't evolve until the last century.

Practice Exercise 7

1. c   2. a   3. a

4. In a recent year, more than eight million bikes were sold in the United States, and a third of them went to adults. The year before, only 15 percent of new bike sales were for adults.

Practice Exercise 8

1. d   2. b   3. a

4. Thousands of feet above, astonished airline pilots saw Manhattan fade, then disappear.

Practice Exercise 9

1. b   2. a   3. d

4. It can be tamed and taught to perform complicated tricks, even to mimic human speech.

Practice Exercise 10

1. c   2. d   3. d

4. Unfortunately, narrow lanes mean less room for drivers to correct their mistakes or inattention, and less room for the swaying of a car in a crosswind. Two cars on narrow lanes may actually touch even though the tires will be within their respective lanes.

Practice Exercise 11

1. a   2. d   3. d

4. They are a salty group of mariners who know the underwater contours lying off the city of San Francisco as well as they know the seamed palms of their hands.

Practice Exercise 12

1. b   2. a   3. b

4. A skilled hunter can bring down an animal at a distance as great as 400 feet, or more than 120 meters.

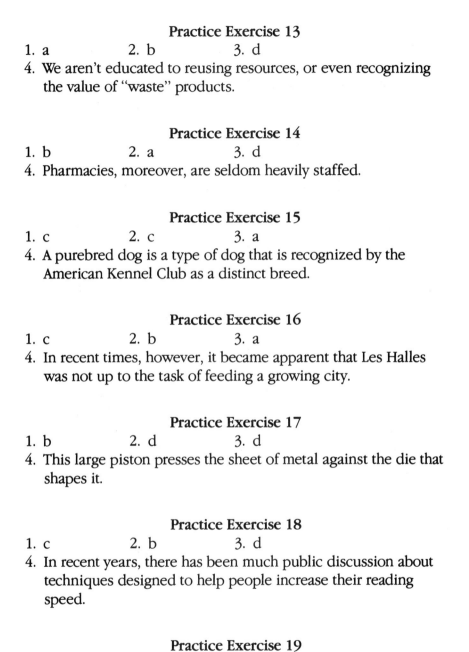

Practice Exercise 13
1. a   2. b   3. d
4. We aren't educated to reusing resources, or even recognizing the value of "waste" products.

Practice Exercise 14
1. b   2. a   3. d
4. Pharmacies, moreover, are seldom heavily staffed.

Practice Exercise 15
1. c   2. c   3. a
4. A purebred dog is a type of dog that is recognized by the American Kennel Club as a distinct breed.

Practice Exercise 16
1. c   2. b   3. a
4. In recent times, however, it became apparent that Les Halles was not up to the task of feeding a growing city.

Practice Exercise 17
1. b   2. d   3. d
4. This large piston presses the sheet of metal against the die that shapes it.

Practice Exercise 18
1. c   2. b   3. d
4. In recent years, there has been much public discussion about techniques designed to help people increase their reading speed.

Practice Exercise 19
1. a   2. c   3. d
4. Edward F. Carpenter, headmaster of "The Prep," as it is known by the students, admits that it isn't easy.

Practice Exercise 20

1. c   2. a   3. b

4. In its own low-key self-promotion, Boston neither brags of its past nor projects some galactic future.

Practice Exercise 21

1. b   2. d   3. d

4. Studies have shown that most injuries and deaths resulting from accidents are caused when people are thrown out of or against the interior of the vehicle.

Practice Exercise 22

1. c   2. a   3. d

4. Treating our waste water *before* it is discharged into lakes, rivers, or the ocean is far less expensive.

Practice Exercise 23

1. b   2. b   3. c

4. The tale became so popular that other novelists, and later the movies, used episodes that depicted a person struggling in the arms of this marine monster.

Practice Exercise 24

1. b   2. a   3. b

4. One water-supply tunnel, explored by modern archaeologists, was driven 3,000 feet (more than 900 meters) through the base of a hill on the Greek island of Samos in the sixth century B.C.

Practice Exercise 25

1. c   2. b   3. b

4. Thanks to the Egyptian climate, we know more about the vanished Egyptians than we know about any other ancient people, much more than we know about the early Greeks and Romans, whose civilizations died just yesterday.

Practice Exercise 26

1. a   2. c   3. b

4. Upon arrival, take it easy. Don't try to adjust to local time schedules all at once.

Practice Exercise 27

1. a   2. a   3. d

4. Put a big telephoto lens on your camera and an alligator catches a fish right under your nose.

Practice Exercise 28

1. a   2. a   3. b

4. Sinister as they may be in the insect world, scorpions devour many varieties of insects that destroy grain fields.

Practice Exercise 29

1. d   2. b   3. b

4. The image of the forester as a rugged woodsman riding guard on national forests is not an accurate picture today. Although outdoor work is still important, forestry today requires management, mathematics, engineering, and human relations skills as well as professional forestry competence.

Practice Exercise 30

1. a   2. c   3. c

4. Today's veterinarians, mostly city-based, not only deal with a broad range of animal diseases but also play a widening role in improving conditions for human health.